# fondue

# fondue

hamlyn

**NOTES**

Medium eggs have been used throughout.

A few recipes include nuts or nut derivatives. It is advisable for those with known allergic reactions to nuts and nut derivatives and those who may be potentially vulnerable to these allergies, such as pregnant and nursing mothers, invalids, the elderly, babies and children, to avoid dishes made with nuts and nut oils. It is also prudent to check the labels of prepared ingredients for the possible inclusion of nut derivatives.

Ovens should be preheated to the specified temperature. If using a convection oven, follow the manufacturer's instructions for adjusting the time and temperature.

First published in Great Britain in 2004 by Hamlyn,
a division of Octopus Publishing Group Ltd
2–4 Heron Quays, London E14 4JP

Copyright © Octopus Publishing Group Ltd 2004

ISBN 0 600 61140 X
EAN 9780600611400

A CIP catalogue record for this book is available from the British Library

Printed and bound in China

10 9 8 7 6 5 4 3 2

# contents

# Introduction

Indulgent, impressive, but above all fun, fondue is not only a delicious meal but a social event in itself. It is the perfect way to entertain friends and family, offering a casual and enjoyable dining experience for all ages. You do the shopping and chopping, and let your guests do the cooking and serving. What could be easier?

## What is fondue?

Fondue is the national dish of Switzerland. The word fondue comes from the French word *fondre* which means 'to melt'. It is traditionally a simple dish of melted cheese which is served in a communal pot, or *caquelon*. Each guest has a long fork on which cubes of bread are speared and dipped into the unctuous cheese. Nowadays, however, the term fondue is used to mean just about any tabletop cooking, and the fondue pot can be filled with broth or hot oil in which small pieces of food are cooked, or any other type of sauce – sweet or savoury – in which items of food are dipped.

## A brief history of fondue

Cheese fondues originated in Switzerland, probably in the Neuchâtel area. The idea dates back to the 18th century when cheese and wine were plentiful, as they are today, and this simple meal was prepared from the ingredients to hand. Most traditional recipes used a combination of Gruyère and Emmental cheeses to get the right balance of flavour. The cheeses were usually melted in a little white wine which helped to prevent them burning and added to the taste. Kirsch was added when the cheese was too bland to produce the desired tartness. Each area of Switzerland had its own style of fondue: for example, in Geneva they also added a third cheese – Walliser Bergkäse – and sometimes mushrooms as well, whereas in eastern areas they used Appenzell and vacherin cheeses melted in cider.

## Equipment

The traditional fondue pot (*caquelon* or *câclon*) is made from earthenware, though today there are ceramic and metal pots available.

For a cheese or dessert fondue, the traditional earthenware pot is a good choice as it tends to be wide and shallow, allowing good heat distribution and easy access for forks. For a broth or oil fondue, select a deep fondue pot which stands securely on a stand over the burner. Some models are rather top-heavy which could be potentially very dangerous. A heavy enamel or other metal pot is a good choice for broth and oil fondues. If you wish to make both types of fondue, select a copper or stainless steel fondue pot with a removable porcelain liner. Use the pot with the liner for cheese and dessert fondues, and remove the liner when you are making a broth or oil fondue. Most fondue pots come with an alcohol burner under the pot to keep the fondue warm, although there are electric models and those which use the solid fuel sterno. Whatever the fuel, make sure the heat source is adjustable so you have control over the temperature. The only other equipment you will need is a set of forks. Fondue forks are long and slim with heat-resistant handles. They usually have two barbed tines, and many have different coloured handles so diners can keep track of their own fork.

## Cheese fondues

Cheese is the original and, for many, the best fondue. In its simplest form, a cheese fondue is made by heating some white wine, adding shredded cheese and stirring until it melts to form a thick sauce. This book dedicates a whole chapter to cheese fondues, including Classic Cheese Fondue served with bacon-wrapped sausages (see page 10), or a Stilton Fondue with Walnuts and Honey, served with pears and walnut bread (see page 21).

### Flavourings

**Cheese** There are many different types of cheeses to try, and different combinations will have different effects. Choose well-aged cheeses for best results; those that melt well include Emmental, Gruyère, Cheddar, Edam, Gouda, fontina, vacherin, Comté, pecorino, and provolone.

**Garlic** Stir in crushed garlic for the full punch or rub the cut side of a garlic clove around the pan before adding the other ingredients for a more subtle flavour.

**Alcohol** Dry white wine is the usual choice, but experiment with cider, beer, brandy, or Champagne. Accompany the fondue with whatever drink you have used in it.

**Other flavours** Sun-dried tomatoes, mustard and fresh or dried herbs make good additions to cheese fondues, or try spices such as cayenne, cumin or caraway.

### Dippers

Just about anything can be dipped into a cheese fondue. Crusty French bread is the classic choice. Cut it into cubes, each with a bit of crust to make it easier to spear. Why not try a selection of different breads to add interest? Cherry tomatoes, grapes, chunks of celery, apple, pear, and mangetouts can all be served raw for dipping and make a pleasant contrast to the creamy cheese. Other vegetables such as broccoli, courgette, and asparagus must be lightly steamed, but are equally delicious. Chunks of ham, sausage or frankfurters could be served alongside.

### Hints and tips for the perfect cheese fondue

- The slower you melt the cheese, the less stringy will be the finished result. So keep the heat low and gently does it.
- When you add the cheese to the simmering wine, stir the pan in a zigzag or figure-of-eight motion to break up the cheese.
- A little lemon juice will help to melt the cheese and make the fondue smoother.
- For a really silky fondue, soak the shredded cheese in cold wine for an hour before cooking.
- To prevent cheese fondues from curdling or separating, toss a couple of teaspoons of cornflour with the shredded cheese before adding it to the fondue.

## Oil and broth fondues

A fondue pot can also be filled with simmering oil or broth into which guests dip small pieces of raw meat, fish and vegetables to be cooked.

### Dippers

Choose pieces of food which will cook quickly. Tender pieces of meat such as fillet steak, lamb, and chicken breast should be cut into cubes or thin slices. Fish and seafood are ideal for fondues as they take little time to cook. Mushrooms, courgette chunks and asparagus are also well worthwhile.

## Sweet fondues

These are a more recent invention and offer a tantalizing dessert choice for a dinner party. Chocolate is perhaps the best-loved, though fruit fondues and other flavours are just as delicious. Try Mocha Fondue with marshmallows and sugar-dipped cherries (see page 53) or Spicy Peach Fondue with griddled panettone and mascarpone (see page 61). Dippers can include chunks of cake, marshmallows, biscuits or fresh fruits.

## Technique and etiquette

As eating fondue is a communal experience, there are a few points of technique and etiquette to consider.

- Spear a piece of bread on a fondue fork, crust last, and dip it in the pot. Twirl the bread gently in the pot to coat it in cheese. A figure-of-eight pattern is best.
- Withdraw the fork and pause with the bread over the pot. This allows the excess cheese to drip back into the pot, and also allows the cheese to cool.
- If you want to be really polite, slide the bread off your fondue fork and onto a dining fork and then into your mouth.
- Tradition states that a small glass of wine should be drunk during the preparation of the fondue and another midway through the proceedings.

1 **garlic clove**, halved

150 ml (¼ pint) **dry white wine**

1 tablespoon **lemon juice**

300 g (10 oz) **Emmental cheese**, grated

300 g (10 oz) **Gruyère cheese**, grated

1 tablespoon **cornflour**

1 teaspoon **mustard powder**

3 tablespoons **kirsch**

**pepper**

To serve

**wrapped sausages, cubes of bread**

*Serves 4*

# Classic cheese fondue

**1** Rub the inside of a fondue pot with the garlic, then discard. Pour the wine and lemon juice into the fondue pot and bring to the boil on the hob, then reduce the heat so that the liquid is simmering. Gradually add the Emmental and Gruyère, stirring continuously, until all the cheese is combined.

**2** Blend the cornflour, mustard powder and kirsch and add to the fondue. Cook gently for 2–3 minutes, then season to taste with pepper.

**3** Transfer the fondue pot to its tabletop burner and serve with the wrapped sausages and cubes of bread.

*Preparation time* **10 minutes**

*Cooking time* **15–20 minutes**

Wrapped sausages

12 rashers **streaky bacon**

24 **mini chipolatas**

1 tablespoon **olive oil**

**1** Stretch the bacon rashers with the back of a knife, then cut each one in half. Wrap the chipolatas in the bacon, secure in place with a cocktail stick, and place in a roasting tin. Drizzle with the olive oil and bake in a preheated oven at 200°C (400°F), Gas Mark 6 for 20–25 minutes until they are golden and cooked through. Remove sticks before dipping.

*Preparation time* **10 minutes**

*Cooking time* **25 minutes**

1 **Camembert**, in a box

1 **garlic clove**, crushed

1 tablespoon **port**

25 g (1 oz) **dried cranberries**

1 teaspoon chopped **thyme**

To serve

slices of **French bread**, toasted

1 small jar of **cranberry sauce**

*Serves 2*

# Baked Camembert with cranberries and port

**1** Take the Camembert out of its box, remove the wrapping then put the cheese back in the box.

**2** Make about 10 holes on the top of the cheese with a small knife. Spread the garlic over the top and drizzle with the port. Gently press the cranberries and thyme on to the rind and replace the lid of the box.

**3** Bake the cheese in a preheated oven at 200°C (400°F), Gas Mark 6 for 25 minutes. Serve in the box with toasted French bread and cranberry sauce.

*Preparation time* **5 minutes**

*Cooking time* **25 minutes**

# Italian cheese fondue

**1** Rub the inside of a fondue pot with the garlic, then discard the garlic. Pour in the wine and lemon juice and bring to the boil.

**2** Over a very low heat, slowly add the mozzarella, pecorino and provolone, stirring continuously until melted. Stir the cornflour mixture into the fondue and simmer for 2–3 minutes until the mixture thickens.

**3** Transfer the fondue pot to its tabletop burner and serve with grissini, salami and a selection of mixed olives.

*Preparation time **8 minutes***

*Cooking time **12 minutes***

1 **garlic clove**, halved

300 ml (½ pint) **fizzy Italian wine**, such as **prosecco**

1 tablespoon **lemon juice**

250 g (8 oz) **buffalo mozzarella cheese**, diced

100 g (3½ oz) **pecorino cheese**, coarsely grated

250 g (8 oz) **young provolone cheese**, coarsely grated

2 tablespoons **cornflour** mixed with 1 tablespoon **water**

To serve

**grissini, salami, mixed olives**

*Serves 4*

50 g (2 oz) **butter**

175 g (6 oz) **leeks**, chopped

175 g (6 oz) **chestnut mushrooms**, sliced

300 ml (½ pint) **cider**

400 g (13 oz) **mature Cheddar cheese**, grated

200 g (7 oz) **Edam cheese**, grated

1 teaspoon **English mustard**

**mini herbed cheese scones**, to serve

*Serves 4*

# Cheese, leek and mushroom fondue

**1** Melt the butter in a fondue pot and fry the leeks on the hob over a medium heat for 3 minutes. Add the mushrooms and cook for around 6 minutes until soft but not coloured.

**2** Pour in the cider and bring to a gentle simmer. Gradually add the Cheddar, Edam and mustard, stirring continuously over a very low heat until melted.

**3** Transfer the fondue pot to its tabletop burner. Serve with mini herbed cheese scones.

*Preparation time **8 minutes***

*Cooking time **20–25 minutes***

**Mini herbed cheese scones**

75 g (3 oz) **butter**

225 g (7½ oz) **self-raising flour**

50 g (2 oz) **Cheddar cheese**, grated

4 tablespoons chopped **mixed herbs**, such as **oregano**, **parsley** or **basil**

1 large **egg**, beaten

4 tablespoons **milk**

**1** Rub together the butter and flour to resemble breadcrumbs. Add the Cheddar, herbs, egg and milk to form a dough. Roll out thickly on a lightly floured surface and cut out 3.5 cm (1½ inch) rounds.

**2** Place the rounds on a lightly greased baking sheet and bake in a preheated oven at 200°C (400°F), Gas Mark 6 for 15–20 minutes until golden brown.

*Preparation time **15 minutes***

*Cooking time **20 minutes***

1 **garlic clove**, halved

200 ml (7 fl oz)
**dry white wine**

2 tablespoons **lemon juice**

300 g (10 oz) **Gouda cheese**, grated

300 g (10 oz) **Romano cheese**, grated

1 tablespoon **cornflour** mixed with 1 tablespoon cold **water**

3 tablespoons **pesto sauce**

**salt** and **pepper**

To serve

**cherry tomatoes, mangetouts**

*Serves 4*

# Cheesy pesto fondue

**1** Rub the inside of a fondue pot with the garlic, then discard. Pour in the wine and lemon juice and bring to a gentle simmer. Gradually add the Gouda and Romano over a low heat and stir until they have melted.

**2** Stir the cornflour mixture into the fondue with the pesto and season to taste with salt and pepper. Simmer gently for 2–3 minutes until the fondue is thick and ready to eat. Transfer the fondue pot to its tabletop burner and serve the fondue immediately with cherry tomatoes and mangetouts.

*Preparation time* **10 minutes**

*Cooking time* **8–10 minutes**

# Smoky cheese and ale fondue

**1** Melt the butter in a fondue pot and fry the onion and garlic over a low heat for 5–10 minutes until soft but not coloured. Stir in the lemon juice.

**2** Pour in the ale and bring slowly to a gentle simmer. Gradually add the smoked Cheddar, stirring continuously until it has melted. Do not boil.

**3** Mix together the mustard, Worcestershire sauce and cornflour and add to the fondue. Cook over a low heat for around 2–3 minutes until thickened. Transfer the fondue pot to its tabletop burner and serve with rosemary and garlic potatoes.

*Preparation time* **10 minutes**

*Cooking time* **25 minutes**

### Rosemary and garlic potatoes

1 kg (2 lb) **floury potatoes**, peeled and quartered

100 ml (3½ oz) **vegetable oil**

1 tablespoon **plain flour** seasoned with **salt** and **pepper**

4 **rosemary sprigs**, chopped

10 **garlic cloves**, skins on, crushed

**1** Cook the potatoes in a pan of boiling water for 8 minutes then drain. Meanwhile, pour the oil into a roasting tin and heat in a preheated oven at 200°C (400°F), Gas Mark 6 for 5 minutes. Sprinkle the potatoes with the seasoned flour and toss to coat evenly.

**2** Put the potatoes into the hot oil and turn to coat. Add rosemary and garlic and roast the potatoes for 45–50 minutes, basting and turning until they are golden.

*Preparation time* **10 minutes**

*Cooking time* **1 hour**

25 g (1 oz) **butter**

1 **red onion**, finely chopped

1 **garlic clove**, crushed

1 tablespoon **lemon juice**

200 ml (7 fl oz) **light ale**

625 g (1¼ lb) **smoked Cheddar** cheese

1 tablespoon **wholegrain mustard**

1 teaspoon **Worcestershire sauce**

1 tablespoon **cornflour**

**rosemary and garlic potatoes**, to serve

*Serves 4*

2–3 tablespoons **chilli oil**

1 **red onion**, chopped

2–3 **Jalepeño chillies**
(fresh or bottled), chopped

1 **red pepper**, cored,
deseeded and chopped

2 teaspoons **Mexican fajita
spice mix**

330 ml (11 fl oz) bottle
**Mexican beer**

juice of ½ **lime**

500 g (1 lb) **Cheddar cheese**,
grated

150 g (5 oz) **cream cheese**

1 small **avocado**, halved,
stoned and diced

To serve

**tortillas, blue corn chips,
refried beans**

*Serves 4*

# Mexican chilli cheese fondue

**1** Heat the oil in a fondue pot and gently fry the onion, chillies and red pepper until soft but not coloured. Add the fajita mix and fry for 1 minute. Pour in the beer and lime juice and bring to a gentle simmer. Add the Cheddar and cream cheese and stir continuously until melted.

**2** Mix in the diced avocado then transfer the fondue pot to its tabletop burner. Serve immediately with crisp tortillas and blue corn chips, a bowl of warmed refried beans and shots of chilled tequila.

*Preparation time **12 minutes***
*Cooking time **10 minutes***

**TIP**
To make tortilla crisps, cut flour tortillas into triangles and fry until crisp. Sprinkle with salt and serve immediately.

1 tablespoon **olive oil**

100 g (3½ oz) **smoked pancetta**, cubed

6 **shallots**, finely chopped

1 **garlic clove**, crushed

200 ml (7 fl oz) **milk**

1 tablespoon **lemon juice**

250 g (8 oz) **mascarpone cheese**

500 g (1 lb) **mature provolone cheese**, grated

¼ teaspoon **ground nutmeg**

**pepper**

**crispy potato skins**, to serve

*Serves 4*

# Cheese and pancetta fondue

**1** Gently heat the oil in a fondue pot and fry the pancetta until golden, add the shallots and garlic and fry gently until softened. Pour in the milk, lemon juice and mascarpone and bring to a gentle simmer. Stir in the provolone and heat gently, stirring continuously, until completely melted.

**2** Stir in the nutmeg and pepper and transfer the fondue pot to its tabletop burner. Serve immediately with the crispy potato skins.

*Preparation time* **10 minutes**

*Cooking time* **10 minutes**

**TIP**
If you have any fondue left over, cover and chill overnight. Spread on a split baguette the next day and place under a hot grill. The cheese will melt and go a crispy golden colour.

Crispy potato skins

8 small **baking potatoes**, in their skins

3–4 tablespoons **olive oil**

30 g (1¼ oz) **Parmesan cheese**, grated

2 teaspoons **paprika**

**pepper**

**1** Bake the potatoes in a preheated oven at 200°C (400°F), Gas Mark 6 for 50–60 minutes. Allow to cool, then cut into quarters and scoop out most but not all of the flesh.

**2** Arrange the skins on a baking sheet, insides up. Sprinkle with olive oil, pepper, Parmesan and paprika and return to the oven for 15 minutes until crispy and golden.

*Preparation time* **8 minutes**

*Cooking time about* **1¼ hours**

# Stilton fondue with walnuts and honey

**1** Rub the inside of a fondue pot with the garlic, then discard.

**2** Pour in the white wine, honey, lemon juice and Madeira and bring to a gentle simmer. Add the Stilton and stir continuously until it has all melted. Mix the cornflour with the yogurt and slowly add the mixture to the fondue. Cook gently for 2–3 minutes.

**3** Stir in the walnuts, chives and pepper, then transfer the fondue to its tabletop burner. Serve immediately with freshly sliced pears and griddled walnut bread.

*Preparation time* **10 minutes**

*Cooking time* **10 minutes**

1 **garlic clove**, halved

150 ml (¼ pint) **white wine**

2 tablespoons **sage honey**

1 tablespoon **lemon juice**

4 tablespoons **Madeira**

625 g (1¼ lb) **Stilton cheese**

1 tablespoon **cornflour**

125 g (4 oz) **Greek yogurt**

75 g (3 oz) **toasted walnuts**, chopped

1 tablespoon snipped **chives**

**pepper**

To serve:

**sliced pears, griddled walnut bread**

*Serves 4*

300 ml (½ pint) **dry rosé wine**

1 tablespoon **lemon juice**

625 g (1¼ lb) **Brie**, rind removed then thinly sliced

1 tablespoon **cornflour**

2 tablespoons **sun-dried tomato paste**

100 g (3½ oz) **sun-blushed tomatoes**, chopped

2 tablespoons chopped **mixed herbs**, such as **oregano, majoram** and **lemon thyme**

**pepper**

**pesto palmiers**, to serve

*Serves 4*

# Brie and sun-blushed tomato fondue

**1** Gently heat the wine and lemon juice in a fondue pot until it reaches a low simmer. Add the Brie and stir continuously until melted.

**2** Mix the cornflour with a little cold water and slowly stir into the fondue. Add the tomato paste, sun-blushed tomatoes and herbs and cook for 2–3 minutes, until rich and thick. Season with pepper then transfer the fondue to its tabletop burner. Serve immediately with pesto palmiers.

*Preparation time* **5 minutes**

*Cooking time* **6–7 minutes**

**Pesto palmiers**
250 g (8 oz) **ready-made puff pastry**

3 tablespoons **pesto sauce**

**1** Roll out the puff pastry to a 20 x 25 cm (8 x 10 inch) rectangle and arrange with the long sides facing you. Spread 2 tablespoons pesto over the pastry then fold both long sides into the middle so that the pesto is covered. Spread 1 tablespoon pesto over the top of the pastry and, again, fold in half lengthways. Turn the pastry 90 degrees and press down gently. Using a sharp knife, cut it into about 25 slices then arrange these slices, cut side up, on nonstick baking sheets, leaving plenty of space to allow for spreading.

**2** Flatten each palmier slightly with the palm of your hand then bake them in a preheated oven at 200°C (400°F), Gas Mark 6 for 10–12 minutes, turning after 8 minutes, until they are crisp and golden in colour.

**3** Remove the palmiers from the oven and cool on a wire rack. You will need to do this in 2–3 batches. The palmiers can be stored in an airtight tin for 2–3 days. Warm them slightly before serving.

*Preparation time* **10 minutes**

*Cooking time* **10–12 minutes** *per batch*

## Lemon mayo fondue

225 ml (7½ fl oz) **mayonnaise**

finely grated rind of 1 **lemon**

1 tablespoon **lemon juice**

4 tablespoons **pine nuts**, lightly toasted

**pepper**

## Crunchy herb asparagus

50 g (2 oz) **butter**

2 tablespoons **olive oil**

1 large **garlic clove**, crushed

2 teaspoons **chilli flakes**

200 g (7 oz) **fresh breadcrumbs**

2 tablespoons chopped **parsley**

2 tablespoons chopped **chives**

2 tablespoons chopped **chervil**

**sea salt** and **pepper**

500 g (1 lb) bundle **asparagus spears**, blanched

2 **heads endive**, separated into leaves

*Serves 4*

# Lemon mayo fondue with crunchy herb asparagus

**1** To make the lemon mayo, mix the mayonnaise, lemon rind and juice and pine nuts, reserving a pinch of lemon rind as well as 1 tablespoon of pine nuts. Season with salt and pepper and spoon into a small bowl and garnish with the reserved lemon rind and pine nuts. Cover and place in the refrigerator.

**2** To make the breadcrumb mixture, melt the butter with the oil in a frying pan. Add the garlic and chilli flakes and fry for 30 seconds then add the breadcrumbs. Fry the crumbs gently, stirring with a wooden spoon so they don't burn. Add the herbs and season with salt and pepper and fry gently until they are golden brown. Transfer to a bowl.

**3** Cook the blanched asparagus spears on a preheated hot griddle until they are hot and charred. Serve immediately with the endive leaves, using the lemon mayonnaise as a fondue and the breadcrumb mixture for sprinkling.

*Preparation time **15 minutes***

*Cooking time **15 minutes***

# Thai-style fondue with sesame sweet potatoes

**1** Mix all the fondue ingredients, except the coriander, in a small saucepan, place over a low heat and simmer gently for 10 minutes to allow the flavours to develop. Stir in the coriander just before you transfer the fondue to a fondue pot on its tabletop burner.

Sesame sweet potatoes

625 g (1¼ lb) **sweet potatoes**, peeled and cubed

3–4 tablespoons **mild chilli oil** or **olive oil**

2 tablespoons **olive oil**

**1** Toss the sweet potatoes in the oil. Place in a roasting tin and cook in a preheated oven at 200°C (400°F), Gas Mark 6 for 30 minutes until softened and beginning to brown. Sprinkle with the sesame seeds, toss well and then return to the oven for 10 minutes until crispy and golden. Serve immediately with the Thai-style fondue.

*Preparation time* **10 minutes**

*Cooking time* **50 minutes**

270 ml (9 fl oz) **coconut cream**

1 large **red chilli**, finely sliced

1 **lemon grass stalk**, thinly sliced

juice of ½ **lime**

2.5 cm (1 inch) cube **root ginger**, peeled and sliced

½ teaspoon **salt**

½ tablespoon **toasted sesame oil**, plus extra to garnish

2 **cardamon pods**, crushed

1 **star anise**

2 tablespoons chopped **coriander leaves**

**sesame sweet potatoes**, to serve

*Serves 4*

50 g (2 oz) **butter**

5 **red onions**, thinly sliced

juice of 1 **lemon**

2 tablespoons **plain flour**

350 ml (12 fl oz) **red wine**

350 ml (12 fl oz)
**chicken stock**

3 tablespoons chopped
**thyme**

**salt** and **pepper**

**Gruyère bread**, to serve

*Serves 4*

# Red wine, onion and thyme fondue

**1** Melt the butter in a large heavy-based pan, add the onions and cook slowly over a low heat, stirring frequently, for about 30 minutes, until very soft.

**2** Add the lemon juice, season with salt and pepper and mix well. Stir in the flour and cook for 1 minute. Gradually pour in the wine and stock, stirring continuously. Bring back to the boil, add the thyme and simmer for a further 30 minutes. Pour into a fondue pot over its burner and serve with freshly grilled Gruyère bread.

*Preparation time **5 minutes***

*Cooking time **1 hour***

**Gruyère bread**

1 medium **baguette**

50 g (2 oz) **Gruyère cheese**, grated

2 tablespoons chopped **thyme**

**olive oil**, for drizzling

**1** Cut the baguette into medium slices, around 1.5 cm (¾ inch) thick, and place on a grill tray. Sprinkle with the grated Gruyère and chopped thyme. Drizzle with a little olive oil and cook under a preheated grill until the cheese has melted and the slices of bread have browned. Serve warm with the red onion fondue.

*Preparation time **5 minutes***

*Cooking time **10 minutes***

# Tandoori tofu fondue

**1** Carefully slice the tofu into cubes and drain any excess liquid. Divide between 4 plates.

**2** Half-fill a fondue pot with the oil, and heat on the hob until the temperature reaches 190°C (375°F), or until a cube of bread turns golden in 30 seconds. Transfer the fondue to its tabletop burner to keep warm.

**3** Combine all the tandoori yogurt ingredients and place in a bowl.

**4** Mix the cornflour with the tandoori masala mix and place in a bowl alongside the portions of tofu. Each diner lightly coats their tofu pieces in the tandoori mix then lowers them into the hot oil with a fondue fork and fries them for about 2 minutes until golden brown. Provide some kitchen paper for mopping up any excess oil.

**5** Serve with the tandoori yogurt, a selection of Indian pickles, lemon wedges and crisp poppadums.

*Preparation time **8 minutes***

*Cooking time about **12 minutes** at table*

500 g (1 lb) **firm tofu**

**vegetable oil**, for deep-frying

100 g (3½ oz) **cornflour**

2 tablespoons **tandoori masala powder mix**

**Tandoori yogurt**

350 g (12 oz) **Greek yogurt**

½ **cucumber**, grated and drained of excess liquid

3–4 **mint sprigs**, leaves removed and chopped

To serve

**Indian pickles, lemon wedges, poppadums**

*Serves 4*

1 tablespoon **olive oil**

1 **red onion**, chopped

2 **garlic cloves**, crushed

2 **red chillies**, deseeded and chopped

5 **red peppers**, cored, deseeded and chopped

100 ml (3½ fl oz) **vegetable stock**

100 ml (3½ fl oz) **dry white wine**

1 teaspoon **Worcestershire sauce** (optional)

**salt** and **pepper**

**polenta-coated bubble-and-squeak cakes**, to serve

*Serves 4*

# Red pepper fondue

**1** Heat the oil in a saucepan, add the onion and cook for 5 minutes until softened. Add the garlic, chillies and red peppers and cook for 4–5 minutes. Pour in the stock and wine, cover the pan and cook over a low heat for 20 minutes.

**2** Tip the pepper mixture into a food processor and whizz until smooth. Season to taste with salt and pepper then pour into a fondue pot. Transfer the fondue to its tabletop burner to keep warm and serve with the bubble-and-squeak cakes.

*Preparation time **15 minutes***

*Cooking time **30 minutes***

**Polenta-coated bubble-and-squeak cakes**

200 g (7 oz) **Savoy cabbage**, finely sliced

350 g (11½ oz) **potatoes**, diced

350 g (11½ oz) butternut squash or **sweet potato**, peeled and diced

1 tablespoon **wholegrain mustard**

50 g (2 oz) **Parmesan cheese**, grated

3 **spring onions**, finely chopped

3 tablespoons chopped **parsley**

50 g (2 oz) **coarse polenta**, sprinkled on a plate

**salt** and **pepper**

**vegetable oil**, for frying

**1** Plunge the cabbage into a saucepan of boiling water for 2 minutes until just cooked. Drain then rinse under cold running water so it cools quickly. Squeeze out any excess water with your hands.

**2** Boil the potatoes and butternut squash for 15–20 minutes or until tender. Drain and mash with the mustard then stir in the cooked cabbage, Parmesan, spring onions and parsley. Season well with salt and pepper and leave to cool.

**3** Shape the mixture into 20 small round cakes. Dip the cakes into the polenta to coat them evenly. Chill for 30 minutes.

**4** Heat the oil in a frying pan and cook the cakes in batches for about 2 minutes on each side until golden. Serve immediately with the red pepper fondue.

*Preparation time* **25 minutes**

*Cooking time* **35 minutes**

625 g (1¼ lb) **plum tomatoes**, skinned and roughly chopped

250 g (8 oz) **cherry tomatoes**

3 **garlic cloves**, chopped

100 ml (3½ fl oz) **olive oil**

1 teaspoon **dried basil**

3 tablespoons chopped **fresh basil**

**salt** and **pepper**

To serve

**garlic-roasted vegetables, flat bread**

*Serves 4*

# Slow-roasted tomato fondue

**1** Place the plum and cherry tomatoes (with their skins on), garlic, olive oil and dried basil in a roasting tin and toss together. Season well with salt and pepper.

**2** Roast the tomatoes in a preheated oven at 200°C (400°F), Gas Mark 6 for 40 minutes until soft and lightly charred. Remove the tin from the oven and mash the tomatoes into the oil with a fork. Stir in the fresh basil and return to the oven for 20 minutes to allow the flavours to infuse and the liquid to reduce slightly.

**3** Pour the sauce into a fondue pot and place over its tabletop burner. Serve with roasted vegetables and flat bread.

*Preparation time **15 minutes***

*Cooking time **1 hour***

**Garlic-roasted vegetables**

2 **yellow peppers**, cored, deseeded and cut into large dice

500 g (1 lb) **cauliflower**, cut into large florets

1 **courgette**, cut into large discs

1 **large sweet potato**, cut into large dice

3 **garlic cloves**, chopped

50 ml (2 fl oz) **olive oil**

**salt** and **pepper**

**1** Divide the vegetables between 2 roasting tins, sprinkle with garlic and season well with salt and pepper. Toss the vegetables in the oil and roast in a preheated oven at 200°C (400°F), Gas Mark 6 for 50 minutes until golden brown. To serve, thread the cooked vegetables on to skewers.

*Preparation time **10 minutes***

*Cooking time **50 minutes***

# Miso vegetable fondue

**1** Put the miso paste into a saucepan and stir in the stock, add the soy sauce and sake and bring to a gentle simmer. Add the mushrooms, green beans and bok choy and simmer gently for 3–4 minutes.

**2** Stir in the beansprouts, bamboo shoots, spring onions and noodles and heat through. Pour into a Chinese fondue pot (*shabu*) and serve immediately. Guests take the vegetables from the soup with their chopsticks and dip them into teryaki sauce or wasabi paste before eating. When the vegetables are finished, pour the stock and noodles into individual bowls and serve as a soup.

*Preparation time* **15 minutes**

*Cooking time* **15 minutes**

2 tablespoons **miso paste**

1 litre (1¾ pint) **clear vegetable stock**, heated

2 tablespoons **soy sauce**

100 ml (3½ fl oz) **sake**

100 g (3½ oz) each of **shiitake mushrooms** and **oyster mushrooms**, halved

150 g (5 oz) **green beans**, cut into 5 cm (2 inch) lengths

500 g (1 lb) **bok choy**, sliced

100 g (3½ oz) **beansprouts**

225 g (7½ oz) can **bamboo shoots**, drained

1 bunch **spring onions**, sliced

150 g (5 oz) **dry ramen noodles**, soaked until tender

*Serves 4*

1 tablespoon **olive oil**

2 **shallots**, chopped

2 **garlic cloves**, crushed

250 g (8 oz) **baby spinach**

75 g (3 oz) **ricotta cheese**

50 g (2 oz) **feta cheese**

4 x **filo pastry sheets**,
42 x 23 cm (16 x 9 inches)

1 **egg**, beaten

**salt** and **pepper**

**vegetable oil**, for frying


To serve

**Greek yogurt, salad leaves**


*Serves 4*

# Spinach and feta filo pastry fondue

**1** Heat the olive oil in a large saucepan and fry the shallots and garlic until soft but not coloured. Add the spinach and cook until wilted. Remove the pan from the heat, pour off any excess liquid and leave to cool. Put the spinach into a bowl, add the ricotta and feta, season generously with salt and pepper and mix well.

**2** Cut each sheet of filo pastry into 4 equal rectangles and keep them covered with a damp cloth until needed. Spoon 1 tablespoon of the spinach mixture on to the narrow end of a rectangle and spread it out slightly. Firmly roll the pastry into a cigar shape, tucking the sides in as you near the end. Seal by brushing the last 5 cm (2 inches) of the roll with a little beaten egg. Repeat with the other pastry rectangles. Cover and chill the filled rolls until needed.

**3** Half-fill a fondue pot with oil and heat gently on the hob until the temperature reaches 190°C (375°F), or until a cube of bread turns golden in 30 seconds. Transfer the fondue pot to its tabletop burner to keep warm. Diners spear the spinach rolls with fondue forks and dip them into the hot oil for about 2 minutes until golden brown and cooked through. Serve with a bowl of Greek yogurt for dipping and a salad.

*Preparation time **30 minutes***

*Cooking time **5 minutes,** plus about **8 minutes** at table*

**TIP**

If you like your food a little more spicy, then add some harissa paste to the yogurt and serve with the spinach pastries.

200 g (7 oz) **salmon**, roughly chopped

300 g (10 oz) **cod**, roughly chopped

2 tablespoons **Thai red curry paste**

finely grated rind of 1 **lime**

1 tablespoon **soy sauce**

1 **egg yolk**

3 tablespoons chopped **coriander leaves**

1 large **red chilli**, deseeded and finely chopped

4 **spring onions**, finely chopped

**vegetable oil**, for deep-frying

To serve

ready-made **sweet chilli sauce**

½ **cucumber**, peeled and sliced into ribbons

4 tablespoons chopped **coriander leaves**

3 **spring onions**, sliced

1 **lime**, cut into wedges

Serves 4

# Thai fish cakes in hot oil fondue

**1** Place the salmon, cod, curry paste, lime rind, soy sauce and egg yolk in a food processor and whizz until well mixed but not completely smooth. Stir in the coriander, chilli and spring onions. With slightly damp hands, shape the mixture into 20 small cakes. Cover and chill for 1 hour.

**2** Half-fill a fondue pot with the oil, and heat on the hob until the temperature reaches 190°C (375°F), or until a cube of bread turns golden in 30 seconds. Transfer the fondue to its tabletop burner to keep warm.

**3** Diners spear the fish cakes with fondue forks and dip them into the hot oil for about 2–3 minutes until golden brown and cooked through. Serve with sweet chilli sauce and a simple salad of cucumber ribbons, coriander and spring onions garnished with lime wedges.

*Preparation time **20 minutes**, plus chilling*

*Cooking time **5 minutes**, plus about **12 minutes** at table*

# Mini kebabs in hot oil fondue with a mango salsa

**1** First make the mango salsa. Combine all the ingredients in a saucepan and heat them very gently until the mango begins to soften. Remove from the heat and spoon into a dish.

**2** Half-fill a fondue pot with the oil and heat on the hob until the temperature reaches 190°C (375°F), or until a cube of bread turns golden in 30 seconds. Transfer the fondue to its tabletop burner to keep warm.

**3** Arrange the tuna and swordfish on a platter with the red and green peppers. Diners spear pieces of fish and pepper and dip them into the hot oil to cook. Serve with the mango salsa and a salad of frisée lettuce.

*Preparation time* **10 minutes**

*Cooking time* **5 minutes**, *plus about* **8–10 minutes** *at table*

**oil**, for deep-frying

250 g (8 oz) **swordfish steak**, cubed

250 g (8 oz) **tuna**, cubed

1 **red pepper**, cut into large squares

1 **green pepper**, cut into large squares

**frisée lettuce**, to serve

**Spicy mango salsa**

1 **small mango**, peeled and chopped

1 **large red chilli**, deseeded and finely chopped

juice of 1 **lime**

½ **red onion**, finely diced

1 tablespoon chopped **mint**

*Serves 4*

100 g (3½ oz) **plain flour**

pinch of **baking powder**

1 **egg yolk**

1 tablespoon **vegetable oil**

100 ml (3½ fl oz) **beer**

**vegetable oil**, for deep-frying

625 g (1¼ lb) **cod loin**, cut
into 3 cm (1½ inch) cubes

**paprika**

**salt** and **pepper**

**lemon wedges**, to serve


**Tartare sauce**

200 ml (7 fl oz) **mayonnaise**

1 tablespoon **capers**,
rinsed and drained

1 tablespoon finely
chopped **gherkins**

2 tablespoons finely
chopped **parsley**

1 **purple shallot**,
finely chopped

1 tablespoon **lime juice**


*Serves 4*

# Beer-battered cod in hot oil fondue with tartare sauce

**1** Whisk the flour, baking powder, egg yolk, oil and beer to a smooth batter. Cover and leave to rest in the refrigerator for 20 minutes.

**2** Half-fill a fondue pot with the oil, and heat on the hob until the temperature reaches 190°C (375°F), or until a cube of bread turns golden in 30 seconds. Transfer the fondue to its tabletop burner to keep warm. Place the batter in a bowl near the hot oil.

**3** Mix all the ingredients for the tartare sauce and place in a bowl. Season the cod pieces with paprika, salt and pepper.

**4** Diners spear the seasoned cod then dip it into the batter, tapping off any excess. It should be cooked in the hot oil for about 3 minutes until golden brown and cooked. Serve with tartare sauce and lemon wedges.

*Preparation time **15 minutes**, plus resting*

*Cooking time **5 minutes**, plus about **15 minutes** at table*

485 g (15½ oz) **can of pineapple in syrup**

50 ml (2 fl oz) **tomato ketchup**

2 tablespoons **light soy sauce**

50 ml (2 fl oz) **rice wine vinegar**

200 ml (7 fl oz) **water**

2 tablespoons **cornflour** mixed with 2 tablespoons **water**

100 g (3½ oz) **sweet mild red peppers from a jar**, finely chopped

**griddled bacon-wrapped scallops**, to serve

*Serves 4*

# Sweet and sour fondue

**1** Drain the syrup from the can of pineapple into a small saucepan. Stir in the ketchup, soy sauce, vinegar and the water. Bring to the boil and stir in the cornflour mixture. Simmer gently for 2 minutes until thickened.

**2** Chop half of the pineapple and stir it into the fondue with the red peppers. Transfer to a fondue pot over its tabletop burner and serve with the griddled bacon-wrapped scallops and the remaining pineapple, if liked.

*Preparation time **10 minutes***

*Cooking time **8 minutes***

### Griddled bacon-wrapped scallops

16 **medium scallops**, roe removed

8 rashers **smoked streaky bacon**

1 tablespoon **olive oil**

1 tablespoon chopped **parsley**

juice of ½ **lemon**

**1** Stretch the bacon rashers using the blunt edge of a knife until they are almost half their length again. Cut them in half and wrap each scallop in half a bacon rasher. Secure with a cocktail stick so that the bacon does not unwrap.

**2** Heat a griddle pan on the hob over a medium-high heat. Drizzle the scallops with the olive oil and fry for 5 minutes, turning until the bacon is crisp. Sprinkle with parsley, drizzle with lemon juice and serve with the fondue.

*Preparation time **10 minutes***

*Cooking time **5 minutes***

# Thai stock fondue with prawn dumplings

**1** Place all the ingredients for the filling in a food processor. Season with salt and pepper and blend until smooth. Place in a bowl and chill for 1 hour or overnight to allow the flavours to develop.

**2** To fill the dumplings, spoon a tablespoon of the filling into the centre of each wonton wrapper. Dampen the edges with a little water, bring them up around the filling and pinch together at the top to seal. Place on a clingfilm-lined tray, cover lightly and chill until required.

**3** Place all the stock ingredients in a saucepan, bring to the boil and simmer gently for 20 minutes. Remove from the heat, cover and then leave to stand for a further 20 minutes. Strain the stock into a fondue pot and stir in the chopped coriander and soy sauce. Bring slowly to the boil then place the fondue pot on its tabletop burner.

**4** Diners dip their dumplings into the stock and cook them for around 3–4 minutes. Serve the dumplings in bowls with some of the stock or on their own with lime wedges and thick sweet soy sauce for dipping, if liked.

*Preparation time **10 minutes**, plus chilling and standing*

*Cooking time **20 minutes**, plus **16 minutes** at table*

## TIP

If you prefer your dumplings crispy then this dumpling recipe works very well with a hot oil fondue – just deep-fry the dumplings for 2–3 minutes until golden. Serve with lime wedges and extra soy. A sweet chilli sauce is also good.

24 **wonton wrappers** or **skins**

4 tablespoons fresh **coriander**

2 teaspoons **soy sauce**

### Filling

300 g (10 oz) **raw prawns**

75 g (3 oz) **belly pork**, minced

2.5 cm (1 inch) piece **root ginger**, peeled and chopped

grated rind of 1 **lime**

pinch of **Chinese five-spice mix**

5 **water chestnuts**, chopped

1 tablespoon **dark soy sauce**

2 teaspoons **Thai fish sauce**

3 tablespoons fresh **coriander**

### Stock

1.2 litres (2 pints) **chicken stock**

2 **kaffir lime leaves**

1 **red chilli**

2 **lemon grass stalks**

juice of 1 **lime**

2.5 cm (1 inch) piece **fresh root ginger**, peeled and sliced

10 **coriander stems**, chopped

*Serves 4*

## Soup

1 large bunch **coriander**

1 litre (1¾ pint) **fish stock**

5 cm (2 inch) piece **fresh root ginger**, peeled and sliced

2 **garlic cloves**, chopped

¼ teaspoon **saffron threads**

## To serve

6 **spring onions**, sliced diagonally

2.5 cm (1 inch) piece **fresh root ginger**, peeled and cut into fine matchsticks

250 g (8 oz) cooked **Japanese short grain rice** (sushi rice)

600 g (1 lb 3 oz) **salmon fillet**, skinned and sliced

*Serves 4*

# Ginger soup fondue with salmon and sticky rice

**1** Roughly chop all the coriander stems and half the leaves, reserving the remaining leaves, and place in a large saucepan with the stock, ginger, garlic and saffron. Bring to the boil and simmer for 15 minutes then remove from the heat. Strain the liquid into a fondue pot and slowly bring back to the boil. Chop the reserved coriander leaves and add to the fondue pot with the spring onions and ginger. Transfer the fondue to its tabletop burner to keep warm.

**2** Serve each diner a bowl of warm rice and a portion of sliced salmon. They dip their salmon into the simmering soup to cook it then place it on their rice and add some of the soup and some coriander, spring onions and ginger.

*Preparation time* **10 minutes**

*Cook time* **15 minutes**, *plus about* **10 minutes** *at table*

# Fondue Bourguinon

**1** Mix together all the marinade ingredients and add the cubed fillet steak. Cover and chill for at least 4 hours. Remove from refrigerator and leave at room temperature for the final hour of marinating.

**2** Remove the steak from the marinade and pat dry on kitchen paper. Divide between 4 plates. Half-fill a fondue pot with the oil, and heat on the hob until the temperature reaches 190°C (375°F), or until a cube of bread turns golden in 30 seconds. Transfer the fondue to its tabletop burner to keep warm.

**3** Serve diners with a portion of meat and let them cook their own steak as they like it. Serve with mustard sauce and creamed horseradish sauce.

**Mustard sauce**

Mix 6 tablespoons **mayonnaise** with 2 tablespoons **wholegrain mustard** and 1 tablespoon chopped **parsley**

**Creamed horseradish sauce**

Mix 2 tablespoons grated **horseradish** with 125 ml (4 fl oz) **crème fraîche.**

*Preparation time **10 minutes**, plus marinating*

*Cooking time about **15 minutes** at table*

750 g (1½ lb) **beef fillet steak**, cubed

**vegetable oil**, for deep-frying

**Marinade**

450 ml (¾ pint) **full-bodied red wine**

1 **onion**, chopped

2 **garlic cloves**, chopped

2 **bay leaves**

2–3 **parsley sprigs**

2–3 **thyme sprigs**

**salt** and **pepper**

To serve

**mustard sauce, creamed horseradish sauce**

*Serves 4*

750 g (1½ lb) lean **lamb fillet**, sliced paper thin (this is easier to do if the lamb is partially frozen)

1.5 litres (2½ pints) **lamb** or **chicken stock**

2.5 cm (1 inch) piece **fresh root ginger**, cut into fine strips

1 **garlic clove**, finely sliced

4 tablespoons **Chinese rice wine** or **dry sherry**

2 tablespoons **Thai fish sauce**

6 **spring onions**, thinly sliced

500 g (1 lb) **spinach**

1 **bunch coriander**, roughly chopped

250 g (8 oz) **rice vermicelli noodles**

**Dipping sauce**

4 tablespoons **light soy sauce**

2 tablespoons **sesame oil**

2 tablespoons **crunchy peanut butter**

2 tablespoons **chilli sauce**

1 **garlic clove**, crushed

1 teaspoon grated **fresh root ginger**

*Serves 4*

# Mongolian lamb stock fondue

**1** Arrange the lamb slices on a large serving platter, cover and set aside.

**2** Heat the stock in a saucepan with the ginger, garlic, wine and fish sauce and simmer for 15 minutes.

**3** Combine all the ingredients for the dipping sauce and divide between 4 small dishes.

**4** Pour the stock into a Mongolian hotpot or a fondue pot and stir in half of the spring onions, spinach and coriander. Place the pot on its tabletop burner and return to the boil.

**5** Using chopsticks (or fondue forks), each diner dips a slice of lamb into the stock to cook, then dips it into their own dipping sauce on the side.

**6** When the meat is finished, add the remaining greens and the noodles to the hotpot and cook for 5–10 minutes. When the noodles are tender, serve as a soup in individual bowls.

*Preparation time* **15 minutes**

*Cooking time* **15 minutes**, *plus about* **10 minutes** *at table*

200 g (7 oz) **fresh breadcrumbs**

finely grated rind of 1 **lemon**

750 g (1½ lb) **veal**, preferably leg, cubed

2 tablespoons **plain flour**, seasoned with **salt** and **pepper**

2 medium **eggs**, lightly beaten

**groundnut oil**, for deep-frying

To serve

**fresh Italian sauce, steamed vegetables**

*Serves 4*

# Veal milanese hot oil fondue

**1** Mix the breadcrumbs with the lemon rind. Toss the veal cubes in the seasoned flour; dip them into the beaten egg and roll them in the breadcrumb mixture until well coated. Divide between 4 plates.

**2** Half-fill a fondue pot with groundnut oil, and heat on the hob until the temperature reaches 190°C (375°F), or until a cube of bread turns golden in 30 seconds. Transfer the fondue to its tabletop burner to keep warm.

**3** Diners cook their veal on fondue skewers for 1–2 minutes in the hot oil. Serve with the fresh Italian sauce and steamed vegetables.

*Preparation time* **10 minutes**

*Cooking time* **5 minutes**, *plus about* **15 minutes** *at table*

**Fresh Italian sauce**

3 tablespoons **olive oil**

2 **garlic cloves**, finely chopped

finely grated rind of 1 **lemon**

400 g (13 oz) **can chopped tomatoes**

½ teaspoon **sugar**

15 g (½ oz) **basil leaves**, torn, plus extra to garnish

**salt** and **pepper**

**1** Gently heat the oil in a small saucepan, add the chopped garlic and cook for about 30 seconds. Add the lemon rind, tomatoes, sugar and basil and season with salt and pepper. Cover and simmer very gently for about 30 minutes until the sauce is rich and thick. Pour into a bowl, garnish with basil and serve with the veal fondue.

*Preparation time* **5 minutes**

*Cooking time* **30 minutes**

750 g (1½ lb) **chicken breast**, cut into strips

1 **garlic clove**, halved

40 g (1½ oz) **butter**

1 **onion**, finely chopped

2 **celery sticks**, finely sliced

25 g (1 oz) **plain flour**

20 g (¾ oz) **dried wild mushrooms**, soaked in 300 ml (½ pint) hot **chicken stock**

150 ml (¼ pint) **white wine**

1 tablespoon chopped **tarragon**

100 ml (3½ fl oz) **crème fraîche**

**salt** and **pepper**

To serve

**warm crusty bread, green grapes**

*Serves 4*

# Chicken with a creamy wine and tarragon fondue

**1** Thread the chicken on to wooden skewers and grill until cooked and golden. Keep warm.

**2** Rub the inside of a fondue pot with the garlic, then discard the garlic. Place the pot on the hob and melt the butter. Add the onion and celery and fry gently until soft but not coloured. Add the flour, stir well and cook for 2–3 minutes.

**3** Drain the mushrooms and strain the soaking liquor through muslin or a fine meshed sieve. Slowly pour the soaking liquor into the fondue pot with the wine, stirring continuously until it thickens. Chop the mushrooms and add to the fondue with the tarragon. Bring back to the boil and simmer gently for 5 minutes.

**4** Stir in the crème fraîche, season with salt and pepper, then transfer the fondue to its tabletop burner. Serve diners a portion of chicken strips to dip into the tarragon sauce. Serve with warm crusty bread and a plate of green grapes.

*Preparation time* **10 minutes**

*Cooking time* **30 minutes**

groundnut oil, for deep-frying

4 **garlic cloves**

1 tablespoon **coriander seeds**

750 g (1½ lb) **lamb fillet**, cubed

**rocket salad**, to serve

**Dipping sauce**

1 tablespoon **chopped rosemary**

1 tablespoon **Dijon mustard**

1 tablespoon **wholegrain mustard**

2 tablespoons **clover honey**

juice of ½ **lime**

1 tablespoon **aged sherry vinegar**

2 tablespoons **rosemary infused oil** or **olive oil**

**salt** and **pepper**

*Serves 4*

# Lamb skewers in hot oil fondue

**1** Combine all the dipping sauce ingredients in a small saucepan and bring to a gentle simmer. Pour into a bowl and cool slightly.

**2** Half-fill a fondue pot with the oil, and heat on the hob until the temperature reaches 190°C (375°F), or until a cube of bread turns golden in 30 seconds. Transfer the fondue to its tabletop burner to keep warm and add the garlic cloves and coriander seeds to flavour the oil.

**3** Give diners a portion of lamb and let them skewer and cook it as they like it. Serve with the warm dipping sauce and a fresh rocket salad.

*Preparation time **5 minutes***

*Cooking time **5 minutes**, plus about **15 minutes** at table*

# Meatballs in hot oil fondue

**1** Drain any excess liquid from the bread and combine it with the remaining ingredients. Season well with salt and pepper. With slightly wet hands, shape the mixture into about 36 small balls. Cover and chill for 1 hour.

**2** Half-fill a fondue pot with the oil, and heat on the hob until the temperature reaches 190°C (375°F), or until a cube of bread turns golden in 30 seconds. Transfer the fondue pot to its tabletop burner to keep warm.

**3** Diners spear the meatballs with a fondue fork and cook them in the hot oil for 3–4 minutes or until browned and cooked through. Serve with the spicy tomato sauce and a green salad.

*Preparation time* **15 minutes**

*Cooking time about* **20 minutes** *at table*

### Spicy tomato sauce

1 tablespoon **olive oil**

1 **onion**, finely chopped

3 **red chillies**, finely chopped

1 tablespoon **garlic purée**

½ teaspoon **ground cumin**

½ teaspoon **chilli flakes**

2 x 400 g (13 oz) **cans chopped tomatoes**

10 **sun-dried tomatoes in oil**, chopped

2 **bay leaves**

**salt** and **pepper**

**1** Heat the oil in a saucepan, add the onion, chillies and garlic and cook for 2–3 minutes until softened. Stir in the cumin and dried chilli and season with salt and pepper. Add the tomatoes and bay leaves and simmer for 25 minutes. Remove the bay leaves before serving.

*Preparation time* **10 minutes**

*Cooking time* **30 minutes**

50 g (2 oz) **stale bread**, broken into small pieces and soaked in 50 ml (2 fl oz) **milk**

250 g (8 oz) **minced beef**

250 g (8 oz) **minced lamb**

1 tablespoon **garlic purée**

4 **spring onions**, chopped

1 small **bunch parsley**, chopped

1 small **bunch basil**, chopped

**salt** and **pepper**

**oil**, for deep-frying

To serve

**spicy tomato sauce, green salad**

*Serves 4*

250 g (8 oz) **dark chocolate** (minimum 70 per cent cocoa solids)

2 tablespoons **dark rum**

15 g (½ oz) **unsalted butter**

2 tablespoons **double cream**

40 g (1½ oz) **stem ginger**, chopped (optional)

To serve

**fresh strawberries, brandy snaps** or **marshmallows**

*Serves 4*

# Dark chocolate fondue

**1** Fill a fondue pot one-third full of boiling water. Place the porcelain liner in the pot and heat gently on the hob. Break the chocolate into small pieces and put them in the pot with the rum, butter, cream and stem ginger, if using. Place over a very low heat, and stir occasionally until the chocolate has melted.

**2** Transfer the fondue pot to its tabletop burner and keep warm over a low heat. Serve immediately with fresh strawberries and brandy snaps or marshmallows.

*Preparation time* **5 minutes**

*Cooking time* **10 minutes**

200 g (7 oz)
**chocolate spread**

2 tablespoons **smooth
peanut butter** (optional)

200 ml (7 fl oz)
**condensed milk**

To serve

warmed **waffles**, dusted with
**icing sugar**

slices of **mango, strawberry**
and **kiwi fruit**

*Serves 4*

# Quick chocolate nut fondue

**1** Fill a fondue pot one-third full of
boiling water. Place the porcelain
liner in the pot and add the
chocolate spread, peanut butter,
if using, and condensed milk.
Heat gently, stirring constantly,
until the fondue is thoroughly
blended and smooth.

**2** Transfer the fondue pot to its
tabletop burner to keep warm.
Serve immediately with warmed
waffles dusted with icing sugar and
slices of fruit.

*Preparation time **10 minutes***

*Cooking time **5 minutes***

# Mocha fondue

**1** Dissolve the sugar in the hot coffee and set aside to cool.

**2** Fill a fondue pot one-third full of boiling water. Place the porcelain liner in the pot and add the coffee, chocolate, cream, vanilla extract and coffee liqueur, if using. Heat gently, stirring occasionally, until the chocolate has melted and the fondue is thick and smooth.

**3** Transfer the fondue pot to its tabletop burner and keep warm over a low heat. Serve immediately with sugar-dipped cherries and marshmallows.

*Preparation time* **5 minutes**

*Cooking time* **10 minutes**

### Sugar-dipped cherries

To prepare the cherries, whisk a small **egg white** until slightly frothy, dip the **fresh cherries** into it and then dip them in a plate of **caster sugar**. Set aside until needed.

### TIP

If you find that your chocolate fondue starts to separate or go grainy, then whisk in 2–3 tablespoons boiling water. This will restore it to a thick glossy mix.

2 tablespoons **caster sugar**

100 ml (3½ fl oz) **hot strong espresso style coffee** or 2 tablespoons **instant coffee** granules dissolved in 100 ml (3½ fl oz) boiling **water**

300 g (10 oz) **plain chocolate** (minimum 70 per cent cocoa solids), grated

100 ml (3½ fl oz) **double cream**

1 teaspoon **vanilla extract**

2 tablespoons **coffee liqueur**, such as **Kahlúa** (optional)

To serve

**sugar-dipped cherries, marshmallows**

*Serves 4*

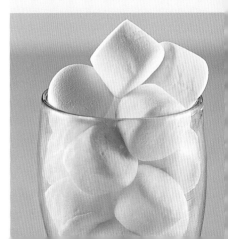

300 g (10 oz) **white chocolate**, chopped

125 ml (4 fl oz) **double cream**

2 tablespoons **Amaretto**

**triple chocolate brownies,** to serve

*Serves 4*

# White chocolate fondue

**1** Fill a fondue pot one-third full of boiling water. Place the porcelain liner in the pot and add the white chocolate, cream and Amaretto. Put the fondue pot on the hob over a very low heat and let the chocolate melt slowly, stirring occasionally.

**2** Transfer the fondue pot to its tabletop burner and keep it warm over a low heat. Serve immediately with the chocolate brownies.

*Preparation time **3 minutes***

*Cooking time **5–10 minutes***

**Triple chocolate brownies**

250 g (8 oz) **plain chocolate** (minimum 70 per cent cocoa solids), roughly chopped

250 g (8 oz) **unsalted butter**, extra for greasing

175 g (6 oz) **plain flour**, extra for greasing

1 teaspoon **baking powder**

pinch of **salt**

300 g (10 oz) **caster sugar**

4 **medium eggs**, lightly beaten

1 teaspoon **vanilla extract**

100 g (3½ oz) **white chocolate**, chopped

100 g (3½ oz) **milk chocolate**, chopped

75 g (3 oz) **pecan nuts**, chopped (optional)

**1** Butter and flour a 30 x 20 cm (12 x 8 inch) baking tin.

**2** Place the plain chocolate and butter in a heavy-based saucepan over a very low heat until melted. Leave to cool a little.

**3** Sieve the flour with the baking powder and salt and set aside. Stir the sugar into the melted chocolate then add the eggs and vanilla essence. Fold in the flour, the white and milk chocolate and nuts, if using.

**4** Pour the mixture into the prepared tin and place in a preheated oven at 180°C (350°F), Gas Mark 4 for 25–30 minutes. Leave to cool in the tin then cut into bite-sized cubes. Store for up to two days in an airtight tin until required.

*Preparation time* **15 minutes**

*Cooking time* **25–30 minutes**

285 g (9½ oz) jar **wild blueberry jam**

300 g (10 oz) **fresh blueberries**

grated rind and juice of 2 **limes**

40 ml (1½ fl oz) **vodka**

1½ teaspoons **cornflour**

**mini cinnamon muffins**, to serve

*Serves 4*

# Blueberry fondue

**1** Place the jam, blueberries and lime rind and juice in a small saucepan, bring to the boil and simmer for 5 minutes. Mix the vodka and cornflour and stir into the blueberry sauce. Bring the sauce back to the boil and simmer for 2 minutes, stirring continuously.

**2** Transfer to a fondue pot over its tabletop burner and serve with the mini cinnamon muffins.

*Preparation time* **5 minutes**

*Cooking time* **10 minutes**

### Mini cinnamon muffins

100 g (3½ oz) **butter**, extra for greasing

150 g (5 oz) **self-raising flour**, extra for dusting

75 g (3 oz) **golden caster sugar**

1 **large egg**, lightly beaten

2 teaspoons **ground cinnamon**

50 ml (2 fl oz) **milk**

**1** Grease two mini muffin tins with butter then dust with a little flour. Cream together the butter and sugar and slowly beat in the egg. Sift the flour and cinnamon together and fold into the mixture with the milk.

**2** Spoon the cinnamon batter into the prepared tins and bake in a preheated oven at 180°C (350°F), Gas Mark 4 for 15–20 minutes. Allow the muffins to cool, then serve with the blueberry fondue.

*Preparation time* **12 minutes**

*Cooking time* **20 minutes**

# Plum and Amaretto fondue

**1** Melt the butter in a small saucepan. Add the red plums, sugar and orange rind and juice and cook over a medium heat for 10 minutes or until the plums start to break up. Mix the Amaretto with the cornflour and stir into the plum sauce. Bring the sauce back to the boil and simmer for 2 minutes, stirring continuously.

**2** Transfer the sauce to a fondue pot and place on its tabletop burner. Serve with slices of almond cake and a bowl of crème fraîche, or cut the almond cake into cubes in order to dip them into the fondue.

*Preparation time* **10 minutes**

*Cooking time* **12 minutes**

### Almond cake

150 g (5 oz) **self-raising flour**

1 teaspoon **baking powder**

175 g (6 oz) **caster sugar**

175 g (6 oz) **butter**, softened

125 g (4 oz) **ground almonds**

3 **large eggs**

50 g (2 oz) **flaked almonds**

4 tablespoons **Amaretto** or **milk**

**1** Lightly grease and line the base of a 900 g (2 lb) loaf tin. Then sift the flour and baking powder into a bowl. Add the sugar, butter, ground almonds and eggs and beat with an electric whisk until smooth.

**2** Spoon the mixture into the loaf tin, level the surface and sprinkle with the flaked almonds. Bake in a preheated oven at 180°C (350°F), Gas Mark 4 for 50 minutes. Serve with the plum fondue.

*Preparation time* **15 minutes**

*Cooking time* **50 minutes**

25 g (1 oz) **butter**

6 **red plums**, stoned and roughly chopped

75 g (3 oz) **golden caster sugar**

rind and juice of 1 **orange**

25 ml (1 fl oz) **Amaretto**

1½ teaspoons **cornflour**

To serve

**almond cake, crème fraîche**

*Serves 4*

100 ml (3½ fl oz) **orange juice**

75 g (3 oz) **sugar**

2 **cardamon pods**, crushed

625 g (1¼ lb) **strawberries**, hulled

50 ml (2 fl oz) **Grand Marnier**


**To serve**

**coconut meringues, mint sprigs, mascarpone cheese** (optional)


*Serves 4*

# Strawberry soup fondue

**1** Heat the orange juice, sugar and cardamon in a small saucepan. Simmer for 2 minutes then remove from the heat and leave to cool.

**2** Place the strawberries in a food processor, strain in the cooled syrup and whizz until the mixture is smooth. Stir in the Grand Marnier, transfer to a freezer container and freeze for at least 3 hours. The soup fondue should be semi-frozen before serving.

**3** Serve the fondue in a glass dish. Place it on a platter piled up with coconut meringues and decorate with mint leaves. You can also serve with a bowl of mascarpone if liked.

*Preparation time **12 minutes**, plus freezing*

### Coconut meringues

3 **egg whites**

150 g (5 oz) **caster sugar**

100 g (3½ oz) **desiccated coconut**


**1** Line a baking sheet with parchment.

**2** Whisk the egg whites until stiff peaks form. Gradually whisk in the sugar. The meringue mixture should be firm and glossy. Fold in two-thirds of the desiccated coconut with a metal spoon and place heaped teaspoons of the mixture on the baking sheet, giving them space to expand slightly.

**3** Sprinkle with the remaining coconut and bake in a preheated oven at 120°C (250°F), Gas Mark ½ for 1¼ hours.

*Preparation time **20 minutes***

*Cooking time **1¼ hours***

50 g (2 oz) **butter**

75 g (3 oz) **light brown sugar**

150 g (5 oz) **golden syrup**

100 ml (4 fl oz) **double cream**

1 tablespoon **lemon juice**

**banana fritters**, to serve

Serves 4

# Toffee fondue

**1** Melt the butter in a small saucepan. Add the sugar and syrup and boil for 2–3 minutes. Remove from the heat and stir in the cream and lemon juice. Bring back to the boil and simmer for 2 minutes, stirring continuously, until slightly thickened. Transfer the toffee fondue to a fondue pot and place on its tabletop burner to keep warm.

*Preparation time* **3 minutes**

*Cooking time* **7 minutes**

**Banana fritters**

125 g (4 oz) **plain flour**

1 tablespoon **oil**, plus extra for deep–frying

175 ml (6 fl oz) **water**

2 **egg whites**

3 **bananas**, cut into large pieces

1 tablespoon **icing sugar** and 1 tablespoon **cocoa powder**

**1** Beat the flour, oil and water until smooth. In a separate bowl, whisk the egg whites until soft peaks form. Fold into the batter mixture.

**2** Half-fill a deep pan with oil and heat until a cube of bread browns in 30 seconds. Dip the bananas into the batter. Fry for 2–3 minutes until crisp and drain on kitchen paper. Dust half the fritters with icing sugar and half with cocoa powder. Serve immediately with the toffee fondue.

*Preparation time* **10 minutes**

*Cooking time* **10–12 minutes**

# Spicy peach fondue

**1** Arrange the peaches so that they are cut side up in a roasting tin. Mix the brown sugar with the allspice and vanilla seeds and sprinkle over the peaches. Drizzle with 3 tablespoons of the peach schnapps and dot with the diced butter. Bake in a preheated oven at 200°C (400°F), Gas Mark 6 for 25–30 minutes until the fruit is tender and caramelized.

**2** Place the peaches in a bowl, cover and set aside for 10 minutes.

**3** Mix the mascarpone with the icing sugar and the remaining peach schnapps. Butter and griddle the panettone.

**4** When the peaches are cool, place in a food processor with the orange juice. Whizz until smooth and pour into a fondue pot over its tabletop burner. Serve with large cubes of griddled panettone and the peach schnapps-flavoured mascarpone cream.

*Preparation time* **10 minutes**

*Cooking time* **25–30 minutes**

6 **ripe peaches**, skinned halved and stoned

4 tablespoons **brown sugar**

½ teaspoon **allspice**

1 **vanilla pod**, halved lengthways and seeds scraped out

5 tablespoons **peach schnapps**

50 g (2 oz) **butter**, diced

250 g (8 oz) **mascarpone cheese**

3–4 tablespoons **icing sugar**

To serve

4–8 slices **panettone**, buttered and then griddled

4–6 tablespoons **orange juice**

*Serves 4*

300 ml (½ pint) **Champagne** or **cava**

1 **egg**

5 **egg yolks**

150 g (5 oz) **caster sugar**

grated rind of 2 **lemons**

To serve

**tuiles, fresh strawberries**

*Serves 4*

# Zabaglione with Champagne

**1** Pour the Champagne into a saucepan and boil rapidly until reduced to 100 ml (4 fl oz). Set aside to cool. Place the egg and egg yolks in a heatproof bowl with the sugar and whisk until doubled in volume.

**2** Place the bowl over a pan of gently simmering water, add the reduced Champagne and lemon rind and whisk for about 8 minutes, until the mixture is very thick and creamy. Serve the zabaglione immediately in a bowl or in individual glasses surrounded by tuiles and fresh strawberries.

*Preparation time **10 minutes***

*Cooking time **15 minutes***

Tuiles

50 g (2 oz) **butter**, melted

50 g (2 oz) **plain flour**

1 **egg white**

65 g (2¼ oz) **caster sugar**

5 **strawberries**, cut into small dice

**1** Grease and flour 2 baking sheets. Beat the egg white until frothy then add the sugar, flour and butter and stir until well mixed.

**2** For each tuile, spoon 2 teaspoons of the mixture onto a prepared baking sheet. Sprinkle with a little diced strawberry and bake in a preheated oven at 200°C (400°F), Gas Mark 6 for 8–10 minutes or until golden.

**3** Remove the tuiles from the oven and while they are still hot place them over a rolling pin. Leave until set then cool on a wire rack.

*Preparation time **10 minutes***

*Cooking time **10 minutes***

**Photography:** Jeremy Hopley

**Food styling:** David Morgan